W9-ASY-828

DISCARDED

Nashville
Public Library
Foundation

*This book
made possible
through generous gifts
to the
Nashville Public Library
Foundation Book Fund*

NASHVILLE PUBLIC LIBRARY

MAGIC

URSULA SZWAST

Heinemann Library
Chicago, Illinois

© 2006 Heinemann Library
a division of Reed Elsevier Inc.
Chicago, Illinois

Customer Service   888–454–2279

Visit our website at www.heinemannlibrary.com

All rights reserved. No part of this publication may be reproduced or transmitted in any form or by any means, electronic or mechanical, including photocopying, recording, taping, or any information storage and retrieval system, without permission in writing from the publisher.

Photo research by Stephanie Miller and Jill Birschbach
Designed by Joanna Turner
Originated by Ambassador Litho Ltd.
Printed in China by WKT Company Ltd.

10 09 08 07 06
10 9 8 7 6 5 4 3 2 1

Library of Congress Cataloging-in-Publication Data

Szwast, Ursula.
  Magic / by Ursula Szwast.
     v. cm. — (Get going! hobbies)
Includes bibliographical references (p.   ) and index.
Contents: What is magic? — Magic, the beginnings — Tips for performing   magic tricks — Helpful equipment — Card tricks — Coin tricks — Close-up magic — Organizations and conventions — Glossary — More books to read and taking it further.
  ISBN 1-4034-6119-8 (Hardcover) — ISBN 1-4034-6126-0 (Paperback)
 1. Magic tricks—Juvenile literature. [1. Magic tricks.] I. Title.
II. Series.
  GV1548.S993 2004
  793.8—dc22
                                        2003025501

Acknowledgments
The author and publisher are grateful to the following for permission to reproduce copyright material: p. 4 Syracuse Newspapers/The Image Works; pp. 5t, 10b, 13, 14, 15, 16, 17, 22, 23 Malcolm Harris/Harcourt Education Ltd.; pp. 11, 18, 19, 20, 21, 24, 25, 26 Robert Lifson/Heinemann Library; pp. 5b, 7 Library of Congress; p. 6 Scala/Art Resource, NY; p. 8 Nancy Sheehan/Photo Edit; p. 9 plainpicture/Alamy; p. 10t Myrleen Ferguson Cate/Photo Edit; pp. 12, 28 Jill Birschbach/Heinemann Library; p.27 Janet Morgan/ Heinemann Library; p. 29 Russell Gordon

Cover photograph of magician and assistant by Royalty-free/Corbis

Special thanks to Mr. Ash, magician and owner of Ash's Magic Shop in Chicago, for his comments that were used to complete this book.

Every effort has been made to contact copyright holders of any material reproduced in this book. Any omissions will be rectified in subsequent printings if notice is given to the publisher.

CONTENTS

Some words are shown in bold, **like this.** You can find out what they mean by looking in the glossary.

WHAT IS MAGIC?

You might have heard the expression "the hand is quicker than the eye." This expression refers to magic. People believe that magicians can do amazing tricks. They pull flowers out of a hat. They know what card a person is thinking about in a deck of cards. Sometimes they even make people "disappear."

This magician, Greg Steele, made it "snow" paper with a trick he performed at a grade school in New York.

Many people think that a magician's hand moves so quickly that the audience cannot follow the moves. The magician's hand, however, is not really quicker than the eye. What magicians do is carefully plan their moves and the words they use to **distract** the audience. They try to get the people in the audience to focus their attention to the wrong place at the right time. This is called **misdirection.**

KINDS OF MAGIC

Magicians perform different kinds of tricks. One kind of magic is called **sleight of hand.** To do these tricks, a magician has to learn skillful hand movements. Most sleight-of-hand tricks involve a deck of cards or coins.

When performing close-up magic, the magician is close to the audience. Sometimes the people surround the magician as he or she performs the magic tricks. Magicians use cards, coins, and other small objects to perform close-up magic.

ILLUSION MAGIC

Illusion is a type of magic that involves large-scale tricks. The performer uses other people, animals, and large equipment. One of the most famous illusions has to do with sawing a person in half. Over the years, this illusion has been performed by several people. Other illusions involve making an object disappear or appear.

Get comfortable handling cards. There are many card tricks to master.

ESCAPE MAGIC

In escape magic, magicians put themselves in situations that appear to be impossible to get out of. For example, they may escape while being handcuffed and in leg irons.

MENTALIST MAGIC

Finally, some magicians perform a type of magic called mentalist magic. These magicians claim to be able to read people's minds and predict events. One mentalist claimed to have read the mind of a person who was underwater in a submarine.

As you can see, magicians perform a variety of amazing tricks. This book will show you how to entertain people using mostly sleight-of-hand and close-up magic tricks.

The magician Harry Houdini performed daring escapes in films and for live audiences.

A HISTORY OF MAGIC

MAGIC IN ANCIENT TIMES

Magic has entertained people throughout history. One of the oldest known **sleight-of-hand** tricks, known as the cups and balls trick, was performed in ancient Egypt in about 2500 B.C.E. The trick was also performed in ancient Greece and Rome.

Records from the first century C.E. show that magicians in ancient times also performed **illusion** magic. One report describes the doors of a temple opening when fires were lit. Another report describes trumpets that sounded without people playing them. Ancient Egyptians, Greeks, and Romans also saw magicians perform at various festivals.

MAGIC IN THE MIDDLE AGES

Magicians continued to entertain people into the **Middle Ages.** In the 1300s, a traveler known as Ibn Batuta wrote about a magic trick he saw in the palace of a Chinese ruler. Ibn Batuta wrote about a juggler who threw a long strap into the air. The juggler then commanded a boy to climb the strap, which he did. This illusion, known as the Indian rope trick, has been reported in other places of the world throughout history.

Hieronymus Bosch made this painting in about 1475. It shows a magician performing a trick.

By the 1500s, magicians throughout Europe entertained people with card tricks and by making all kinds of objects disappear. A magician of that time was named Boccal. Accounts of Boccal's magic describe a trick in which he asked for a bottle of wine and popped the cork. He emptied the bottle and threw the cork into a nearby body of water. The cork later reappeared on a string around the neck of an audience member!

MODERN MAGIC

John Henry Anderson, from Scotland, performed his magic tricks throughout the United States and other countries in the mid-1800s. One of the tricks he is best remembered for is appearing to catch a bullet from a gun fired by a member of the audience.

In the mid-1800s, the famous French magician Jean-Eugène Robert-Houdin entertained audiences with his illusion tricks. Robert-Houdin is thought to be the first great modern illusionist. He became known as the father of modern magic. He also inspired Eric Weisz, who is better known by his stage name—Harry Houdini.

FAMOUS MAGICIANS

Harry Houdini was a famous American escape magician. He seemed to be able to free himself from seemingly inescapable situations. His fame as an escape artist spread throughout the world. By 1900, crowds filled his shows in theaters everywhere. One of Houdini's most astonishing tricks, the Chinese Water Torture Escape, involved him escaping from an airtight tank filled with water.

Today, the magician David Copperfield is famous for both his sleight-of-hand tricks and illusion stunts. He performs hundreds of live shows throughout the world as well as on television specials. He is famous for spectacular outdoor illusion tricks. In one such trick he made the Statue of Liberty "disappear."

This poster advertised a trick in which Houdini was going to escape from being buried alive in a coffin. He died in 1926 before he could perform the trick.

TIPS FOR PERFORMING MAGIC TRICKS

Performing magic tricks for an audience can be a lot of fun. You do not need a special place to perform. A living room, classroom, or theater stage are all good places for you to showcase your talents.

PREPARING YOUR ACT

Before you host a magic show, you want to know how to perform several magic tricks. But the number of tricks you know is not as important as how well you perform them. It is better to perform just a few tricks well instead of many tricks poorly.

Of course, to become a good magician, you have to practice your tricks. The more you practice, the better you will be. You want to make your tricks as **deceptive** as possible. Getting the **timing** right will help you do this. Setting up a **patter** will also help. When you perform a magic trick, what you say is just as important as what you do. It becomes part of the **misdirection** required to fool your audience.

Once you master a few tricks, you could perform a short magic show for your friends or classmates.

It is a good idea to write down what you want to say while performing your tricks. Then memorize it and use it during your act.

A good way to improve your tricks is to practice them in front of a mirror. You might also videotape yourself and then watch the tape to see which parts of your act need improvement.

KEEPING YOUR AUDIENCE'S ATTENTION

When performing your magic, your main task is to keep your audience's attention. It is important to use misdirection to **distract** the people in the audience to keep them from noticing what you are really doing. A good magician never performs a magic trick without practicing it until it can be presented without hesitation. To grab the audience's attention, start out with a simple yet eye-catching trick. Use your longer tricks in the middle of your act. Then finish the act with your most amazing trick.

You will be able to keep up the deception by following some simple rules that all magicians follow. First, never tell your audience how to do a trick. Second, do not do the same trick more than once in a performance. Doing it more than once might give the people a chance to figure out how you did the trick.

This young magician made a hat hover in midair!

To make your act even more **impressive,** you might want to wear a costume. The kind of costume you create is up to you. A magician's vest, cape, or top hat can help you look the part.

You will need a few pieces of equipment to perform many of your magic tricks. You probably will find most of the things you will need in your own home.

CARDS

Many **sleight-of-hand** tricks use playing cards, so a deck of cards is an important part of your equipment. Have several complete decks available.

*This boy chose a **traditional** magician's hat and cape to complete his costume.*

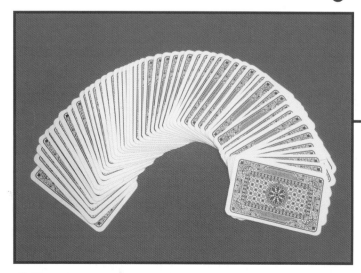

A full deck of cards has 52 cards.

MAGIC WAND

A wand can add a special touch to your magic tricks. You can buy a wand, or make one and decorate it. A scarf or a large handkerchief can help create the **deception** you need in some of your tricks.

You could buy a wand like this in a store, or make your own wand out of a stick or cardboard.

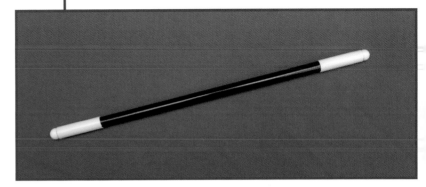

CUPS AND BALLS

Cups and balls were used in one of the earliest known magic tricks. These can be helpful in performing several different magic tricks.

You can use ordinary plastic cups and rubber balls from a store to perform cups and balls tricks.

COINS

Coins are also used in many magic tricks. You can use coins you have on hand or ask for **volunteers** from the audience to contribute coins.

Quarters are a good-sized coin to use in sleight-of-hand tricks.

Some of the most popular magic tricks are card tricks. Here are some tricks that you can add to your magic act.

THE ABRACADABRA TRICK

You will need:
21 randomly chosen cards from a deck of cards

1 Deal the 21 cards, face up, into three **columns** by dealing seven **rows** of three. Deal the cards starting at your left and dealing to the right. The photo on this page shows how the cards should look.

2 As you are dealing the cards, tell the audience what you are doing.

3 Choose someone from the audience and tell him or her to think of any card in one of the columns. Tell the audience member to remember the chosen card but not tell you what it is.

4 Ask the person to tell you which column the card is in.

5 Pick up the cards in one of the columns, then the column that the volunteer's card is in, and then the last column. You must pick up the cards one card at a time starting at either the top or the bottom of each column. The cards should remain face up until step 14. Place each new card at the bottom of the pile in your hand. The column of cards that has the chosen card should be between the other two columns of cards.

6 Deal the cards out again, just like you did in step 1.

7 Ask the same person from the audience to tell you which column the card is in this time.

8 Repeat step 5.

9 Deal the cards a third time, and have the audience member tell you which column the card is in now.

10 Repeat step 5.

11 Now it's time to find the card.

12 Hold the cards face down in your hand. Ask the volunteer if he or she has ever heard the word ABRACADABRA.

13 Tell the audience that ABRACADABRA is a magic word that you will use to find the card. Flip the pile of cards over in your hand and hold the cards face down.

14 Spell ABRACADABRA out loud and deal one card for each letter in the word. Deal the cards face down, starting from the top of the pile. When you get to the last A of the magic word, turn over that card. That card will be the chosen card.

THE FOUR ACES TRICK

You will need:
a deck of cards

1 Before you start your trick, place four aces, face down, on top of the deck.

2 Place the deck of cards on the table. Ask a volunteer to cut the deck into four piles.

3 While the volunteer is cutting the deck, be aware of which pile has the aces.

4 Pick up one pile, but not the pile with the aces. That pile should be picked up last. Take three cards from the top of the pile you picked up and place them on the bottom of the pile.

5 Then take three cards from the top of this pile. Place one card on top of each of the other three piles.

6 Repeat steps 4 and 5 with the other three piles. Handle the pile with the aces last.

7 When you have finished handling all four piles, ask a volunteer to turn over the top card of each pile.

8 The volunteer should find that all four cards are aces!

ANOTHER GREAT CARD TRICK

You will need:
a deck of cards

1 Look at the bottom card of the deck before you start this trick. You have to remember this card.

2 Ask a **volunteer** to cut, or separate, the deck into five piles.

3 Ask him or her to choose the top card of one of the piles, look at it, and remember that card.

4 Pick up all five piles of cards. Make sure you place the pile with the bottom card that you remembered on top of the pile that has the card that the volunteer chose. That will place the volunteer's card immediately next to your memorized card.

5 If the volunteer chooses the top card of the pile that has the card you remembered, tell the volunteer to cut the pile. Then complete the cut, placing the part of the pile with your memorized card on top of the other part.

6 Then put the other piles together in any order.

7 Now tell the audience that you will find the card the volunteer chose.

8 Hold the deck of cards face down in your hand. Starting with the top card, place each card face up until you find your memorized card. The card that you place face up next will be the card the volunteer chose.

9 Point to that card as proof of your magical powers.

Don't forget the card that you memorize. It is the key to knowing which card your volunteer picked.

COIN TRICKS

SWITCH THE COIN TRICK

You will need:
two coins

1 Ask a volunteer in the audience for two coins. If no one offers, provide two coins of your own.

2 Place one coin in each palm. Place the coin in your left hand just below the fingers, near your thumb.

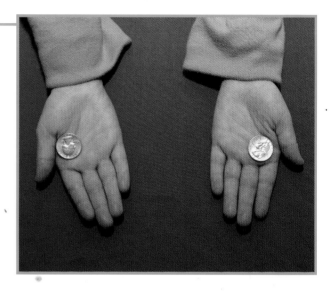

3 Place the other coin in your right hand near your thumb. Show your palms to the audience.

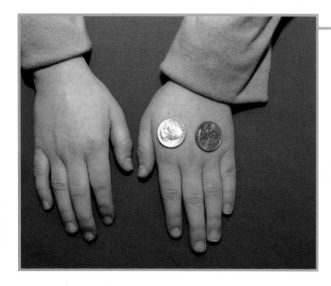

4 The next step has to be done quickly and precisely. At precisely the same time, turn both hands over quickly so the thumbs come close together. As you make this move, toss the coin in your right hand under the left hand.

The purpose of the above photo is to show that both coins should be under your left hand after you complete step 4.

5 If you do this precisely, the people in the audience will think that you only turned your hands over. They will expect to see a coin under each hand.

6 Lift up your right hand. Tell the audience that your magic has made the coin disappear from under your right hand.

7 Then lift up your left hand. Tell the audience that your amazing powers have made an extra coin appear under your left hand.

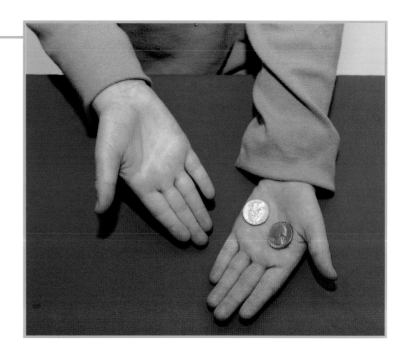

THE KING OF COINS

Coin tricks have been performed for hundreds of years. One performer, T. Nelson Downs, became known as the King of Coins because he specialized in coin tricks and amazed audiences with them. Two of his books are considered excellent guides to help magicians master **sleight-of-hand** magic.

In 1900, he published a book called *Modern Coin Manipulation.* In the book he revealed how to perform several of his famous coin tricks. One trick called "The **Miser's** Dream" resulted in a shower of coins being rained down upon the magician. He published *The Art of Magic* in 1921.

COIN IN POCKET TRICK

You will need:
a coin
a large handkerchief
a shirt or jacket with a breast pocket

1 Hold a coin between the thumb and index finger of your left hand. Keep your hand chest-high, about 18 inches (46 cm) in front of your body.

2 Hold the handkerchief in your right hand and cover the coin.

3 Pull the handkerchief toward your body so that your right hand rests evenly with the pocket on your shirt or jacket.

4 Keep pulling the handkerchief so that the audience can see the coin again.

5 Now repeat steps 1 to 3. But this time, when your right hand meets your left hand, grab the coin between your right index finger and thumb. Keep moving the handkerchief toward you, but be **deceptive** and do not let the audience see what you are doing. Keep the coin covered with the handkerchief at this point.

6 Keep moving your right hand and the coin covered by the handkerchief toward your pocket.

7 When your hand gets near your pocket, let the coin drop into it.

8 Keep moving the handkerchief over the left hand and show that the coin has disappeared!

9 Show your audience that both of your hands are empty. Tell them to check the empty handkerchief.

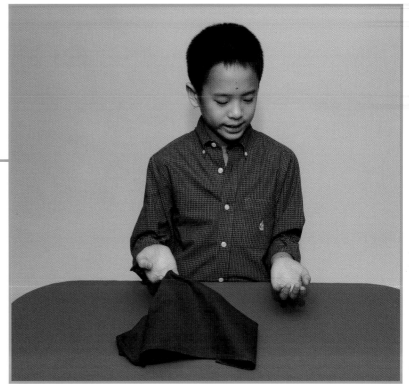

TRICK TIPS

1. Practice all your tricks in front of a mirror so you see your tricks in the same way the audience does. Practice as much as you can.
2. Practice your **patter**, or what you will say during your performance.
3. Try not to tell how tricks work. The audience will be more impressed.
4. Borrow items to use in your tricks from the audience. This makes it seem like the magician could not do anything sneaky to the items.

PAPER CLIP TRICK

You will need:
a dollar bill
two paper clips

1 Show the audience a stretched-out dollar bill.

2 Fold the left third of the dollar bill to the right. Place a paper clip from the top of the bill over this part to hold it in place, as shown in the photo. The clip should fit directly over the number value shown on the bill.

3 Turn the dollar bill over so that you are looking at the other side and the clip is at the top. Do not turn the bill upside down.

4 Fold the left end of the bill over to the right to the folded part.

5 Place a paper clip on the dollar bill from the top. Clip together only the two front folds of the bill. The clip should be placed over the number value, as shown in the photo on the right.

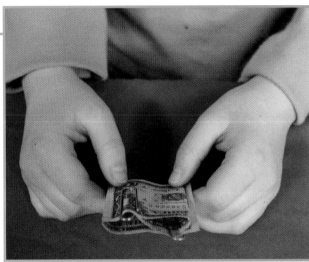

6 Now tightly hold the ends of the dollar bill as shown in the photo. Start pulling the ends apart.

7 When the clips are almost next to each other, sharply pull apart the ends of the bill. The paper clips will shoot toward you and they will be linked together.

8 Point out your magic powers to the audience!

KNOT TRICK

You will need:
a three-foot (one-meter) piece of thin rope
a piece of magician's wax (available at magic trick stores and some hobby stores) or a small piece of white glue stick

1 Before you start, stick a small piece of the wax or glue stick about two-thirds of the way down the rope. The audience should not see you do this.

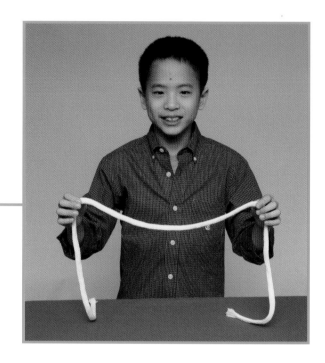

2 Hold the rope outstretched with both hands. The part with the wax or glue should be facing you.

3 Keep your right hand still while you move the rope with your left hand to the right. Stick a piece of rope on the wax or glue. Press the rope hard with your right thumb to keep it in place.

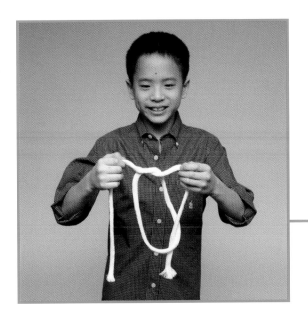

4 Use the middle finger of your left hand to pull the piece of rope that is hanging through the loop. This should look as if you have made a knot. Hold this out for the audience to see.

5 Tell the audience that you will now perform the magic.

6 Move both wrists outward and the rope will fly up. The "knot" will have disappeared.

7 Point out your magical skills to everyone in the audience.

CUPS AND BALLS TRICK

You will need:
three paper or plastic cups
two paper, rubber, or plastic balls (You can make the balls from tissue paper, but it is important that they are all the same size.)
a magic wand

1 Place the three cups, one on top of the other, after you hide one of the balls in the cup in the middle.

2 Put the stack of cups on the table and put the remaining ball in front of you on the table.

3 Pick up the cups, with the mouths facing up. Pull off the cup closest to you and point the cup slightly toward the people in the audience. Do not let the people see completely inside the cup. Then place the cup mouth down on the table. Move smoothly when you do this.

4 Pull off the next cup, and point it slightly away from the audience so that they do not see the ball that you placed inside. Turn the cup mouth down on the table to the right of the first cup. The ball you hid will now be under this cup. Make sure your moves this time look the same as they did when you pulled off the first cup.

5 Take the last cup and point it slightly toward the audience, using the same smooth movements you used with the two other cups. Place the cup mouth down to the right of the other two cups.

6 Pick up the ball that is on the table. Place it on top of the cup that is in the center.

7 Ask the people in the audience where the ball is. They should tell you it is on top of the cup.

8 Tell them that you will use your magic powers and show them that the ball is not on the top of the cup but on the bottom.

9 Place the cup on your right on top of the ball and the center cup. Then place the cup on the left on top of these cups. Take your magic wand and tap the stack of cups.

10 Then lift up the stack of three cups to show that there is a ball under the bottom cup. Tell the audience that your magic power has pushed the ball through the cup.

Visit magic shops like this one to find out about the magic clubs located near you.

There are many ways that you can learn more about doing magic tricks. One way is by finding information in the variety of books about magic tricks. Stores that specialize in equipment for magicians are good places to find out about magic tricks. You can also find equipment that can help you make your performance more interesting and fun.

SOCIETY OF AMERICAN MAGICIANS

The Society of American Magicians (SAM) is the oldest organization for magic in the world, formed in 1902. This organization has more than 7,000 members. The organization works to show magic as a way to entertain. SAM has a special program for young people called the Society of Young Magicians (SYM). This organization has more than 1,000 members, ages seven to fifteen.

INTERNATIONAL BROTHERHOOD OF MAGICIANS

The International Brotherhood of Magicians is the world's largest organization for magicians. It started in 1922, and today has more than 14,000 members. It is a well-respected organization for both **amateur** and **professional** magicians.

THE MAGIC CIRCLE

One of the most **prestigious** organizations in the world of magic is The Magic Circle, formed in 1905. It is based in London, England. The Magic Circle has about 2,000 international members in 38 countries. Members are dedicated to promoting the art of magic.

This 100-year-old organization has the largest membership of professional magicians. It is the only magic organization with various degrees of memberships. One of the highest honors that a magician can earn, called the Member of the Inner Magic Circle with Gold Star (MIMC), is awarded to a select few magicians each year. Only 250 magicians can hold such an honor. It is awarded based on skill and continued dedication to the advancement of magic. The Magic Circle also has a special program for young people called the Young Magicians Club (YMC). This organization has more than 1,000 members, ages seven to seventeen.

CLUBS AND CONVENTIONS

Both the Society of American Magicians and the International Brotherhood of Magicians have clubs in cities throughout the world. These organizations also publish magazines that feature articles that are of interest to all levels of magicians. They hold regular meetings in many cities across the United States and Canada. At these meetings, magic lovers of all skill levels gather to share magic ideas and teach each other new tricks. Young members are encouraged to attend and learn how to become better performers.

The organizations also hold **conventions.** Magicians at the conventions give **lectures** about and demonstrate new tricks to the audience. People who sell equipment and supplies for magicians also attend the conventions to display their items.

If you are interested in performing magic tricks, there are many places and people who can help you with your hobby. They can help you become a better magician, which will help you have more fun performing your tricks.

After a few years of practice, you could put on your own shows like this magician.

GLOSSARY

amateur — person who does something for enjoyment rather than for money

column — vertical, or up-and-down, arrangement of items

convention — gathering of people who meet for a common reason, such as to discuss magic and magic tricks

deceptive — meant to mislead

distract — to draw away the attention of

illusion — type of magic that involves presenting misleading images or events

impressive — having the power to impress, or move or affect people strongly

lecture — talk given before audience or students to educate the listeners

Middle Ages — time in European history from about 500 to about 1450

misdirection — process of focusing audience attention to a place or spot that hides what the magician is actually doing

miser — person who lives poorly in order to save and store money

patter — talk that entertainers use while performing routines

prestigious — very important in the eyes of other people

professional — person who takes part in an activity for money rather than for fun

row — series of things arranged in a horizontal, or side-to-side, line

sleight of hand — type of magic that involves using skillful hand movements

timing — ability to select the precise moment for doing something in order to achieve maximum effect

tradition — handing down of beliefs, customs, or information from one generation to the next

volunteer — person that willingly offers to do something

MORE BOOKS TO READ

Bull, Jane. *The Magic Book.* New York: Dorling Kindersley, 2002.

Eldin, Peter. *Magic with Cards.* Brookfield, Conn.: Millbrook Press, 2000.

Robinson, Richard. *Science and Magic in the Living Room: Amazing Tricks with Ordinary Stuff.* New York: Simon and Schuster Children's Publishing, 2001.

Tocci, Salvadore. *Experiments with Magic.* New York: Scholastic Publishing, 2004.

TAKING IT FURTHER

Houdini Museum
1433 N. Main Ave.
Scranton, PA 18508
(570) 342-5555

International Brotherhood of Magicians
11155 South Towne Square
Suite C
St. Louis, MO 63123
office@magician.org

The Magic Circle
Center for the Magic Arts
12 Stephenson Way
London, England
NW1 2HD
MeetTheMagicCircle
@TheMagicCircle.co.uk

Society of American Magicians
Society of Young Magicians
P.O. Box 510260
St. Louis, MO 63151